THE AI SHIELD

AI CYBER THREATS AND DEFENSE STRATEGIES

PARVEZ KERSI CHHAPGAR

Made with ♥ on the Notion Press Platform
www.notionpress.com

Contents

Preface

The Dawn of a New Digital Era

For a long time, the word "cybersecurity" felt like something that only belonged in corporate boardrooms, government agencies, or the glowing screens of Hollywood hackers. If you had a strong password and some basic antivirus software, you were generally safe. But the rules of the game have changed.

We have crossed the threshold into the age of Artificial Intelligence. AI is undeniably one of the greatest technological marvels of our time, curing diseases, writing code in seconds, and connecting us in ways we never thought possible. However, like any powerful tool, it is a double-edged sword. The same technology designed to make our lives easier is now being weaponised to launch hyper-precise, automated, and devastatingly convincing cyber-attacks.

Today, the hacker is no longer just a person in a dark hoodie guessing your password; it is an intelligent algorithm capable of perfectly cloning a loved one's voice, drafting a flawless phishing email tailored to your deepest interests, or automatically finding the weak points in your home network.

I wrote *The AI Shield – AI Cyber Threats and Defence Strategies* because I realised a critical gap existed. The threats are evolving at a breakneck pace, but public awareness is lagging. I wanted to write a book that my own children, my parents, and my colleagues could read and understand.

This book is not written to scare you; it is written to prepare you. Fear comes from the unknown, but confidence comes from understanding. In the chapters ahead, we will pull back the curtain on how AI is used by cybercriminals, explore real-life scenarios that could happen to any of us, and most importantly, equip you with the "digital armour" needed to protect yourself and your loved ones.

You do not need to be a computer scientist to be safe in the AI era. You just need the right shield. Welcome to the new frontier.

— Parvez K Chhapgar

ACKNOWLEDGEMENTS

Writing a book is a journey rarely undertaken alone, and *The AI Shield* is a true testament to the village that stands behind me.

My deepest gratitude goes first to my parents. Your unwavering support, the strong values you instilled in me, and your endless encouragement have been the steadfast foundation of my life and every milestone I reach.

To my wonderful wife and our children: thank you from the bottom of my heart. My **wife** (Shridevi) for her unwavering support, patience, and belief in me throughout the writing process. My **children** (Tanaz and Ruzbeh) for being a source of joy, inspiration, and motivation. Your boundless love, immense patience, and daily motivation were my ultimate anchors, especially during the long hours and quiet sacrifices required to bring this book to life. You are my greatest inspiration.

I also extend my sincere appreciation to the mentors and leaders whose guidance and professional influence have profoundly shaped my career and my thinking. A special thank you to Animesh Doshi, Benjamin Brahmne, Gaurav Batra, Prashant Phatak, Prasad Shitole, Sunir Thakkar, Scott E. Augenbaum, Varrun Sachdev, and Wouter Goderis. Your profound insights, exceptional leadership, and steady encouragement were instrumental in refining my vision and carrying this work through to completion. You have consistently challenged me to grow.

Grateful to the Be10X team and all the trainers for their support and knowledge they shared in my journey to upskill myself in AI tools, techniques and technology.

Finally, to every friend, colleague, and well-wisher who supported this journey, whether directly or indirectly, thank you. Your belief in my purpose made all the difference.

About The Author

Parvez Kersi Chhapgar is a seasoned cybersecurity professional, technologist, and passionate educator dedicated to making the digital world a safer place for everyone. With 27 years of experience navigating the complex landscapes of technology and information security, Parvez has witnessed first-hand the dramatic evolution of cyber threats from simple viruses to today's highly sophisticated, AI-driven attacks.

Driven by the belief that cybersecurity should not be confined to IT departments, Parvez specialises in breaking down complex technical concepts into accessible, actionable knowledge for everyday people. *The AI Shield* was born out of a personal mission to empower families, teenagers, and seniors alike to navigate the new digital frontier with confidence and peace of mind.

When not dissecting the latest cyber trends or mentoring the next generation of tech leaders, Parvez enjoys movies, horse riding, and rifle shooting. He lives in Pune with his wife and children, who remain his greatest inspiration and the ultimate reason he fights for a safer digital tomorrow.

List Of Sources Used (The AI Shield)

Writing a book that spans the rapidly evolving fields of Cybersecurity and Artificial Intelligence requires synthesising data from countless sources, ranging from academic papers to breaking news reports. "The AI Shield" is built upon the foundational knowledge and specific examples provided by the following institutions, organisations, and research bodies.

I. Government and International Organisations (Threat Intelligence & Defence Frameworks)

CISA (Cybersecurity and Infrastructure Security Agency): Essential for understanding the landscape of critical infrastructure threats, vulnerability management, and defensive best practices (CISA.gov).

ENISA (European Union Agency for Cybersecurity): Provided crucial frameworks for digital identity, risk management, and the EU perspective on AI and cyber risk (ENISA.europa.eu).

NIST (National Institute of Standards and Technology): Specifically, the Cybersecurity Framework (CSF) and the emerging AI Risk Management Framework (AI RMF), which provided the structural backbone for our defence strategies (NIST.gov).

Europol & INTERPOL: Crucial for analysing the methods of transnational cybercriminal networks, particularly in relation to modern fraud, BEC scams, and ransomware (Europol.europa.eu, INTERPOL.int).

National Cybersecurity Alliance: Sources for data on consumer awareness, social engineering metrics, and public defence habits (staysafeonline.org).

II. Academic Institutions & Research Labs (AI Theory & Ethics)

Stanford University Human-Centred AI (HAI): Key studies on the capabilities and limitations of large language models (LLMs) and the long-term ethical risks of AI deployment.

MIT Computer Science and Artificial Intelligence Laboratory (CSAIL): Fundamental research into machine learning, deepfake generating, and adversarial AI techniques.|

Carnegie Mellon University (CMU) CyLab: Critical research on IoT security, privacy governance, and algorithmic fairness.

The AI Now Institute (NYU): Key sources for data on data privacy, surveillance, and the social impact of algorithmic decision-making.

III. Industry Leaders & Security Corporations (Threat Data & Case Studies)

Microsoft Threat Intelligence (Microsoft Security): Deep reports on nation-state actors, widespread phishing campaigns, and the practical application of AI in SOC operations.

Google Threat Analysis Group (TAG): Crucial data on Zero-Day exploits, malware analysis, and the security implications of advanced AI integration into consumer products.

Check Point Research & Sophos Labs: Essential reports on ransomware trends, mobile security, and the mechanics of modern social engineering.

CrowdStrike & Palo Alto Networks: Deep technical insights into endpoint protection, network defence, and managed detection and response (MDR).

Verizon Data Breach Investigations Report (DBIR): The definitive source for multi-year trends in attack patterns, impact, and victim demographics.

IV. Foundations and Think Tanks (Data Privacy & Tech Policy)

The Electronic Frontier Foundation (EFF): Essential resources on privacy law, data sovereignty, and the impact of technological surveillance.

The Centre for Strategic and International Studies (CSIS): Strategic analysis of cyber warfare, global tech competition, and national security implications of AI.

Future of Privacy Forum (FPF): Guidance on data privacy governance, corporate data ethics, and consumer protection law (GDPR, CCPA).

OECD (Organisation for Economic Co-operation and Development): International perspective on digital economy governance and the development of responsible AI principles.

V. Major Media and Technology Reporting (Case Studies and News)

The writing of "The AI Shield" also relied on thousands of data points and case studies derived from dedicated cybersecurity news outlets, including *The Hacker News*, *Dark Reading*, *Wired (Security)*, *TechCrunch*, and the dedicated technology desks of *The New York Times*, *The Washington Post*, and *The Wall Street Journal.*

Part 1: The New Frontier - Why Hackers Love AI

Welcome to the beginning of your journey. To understand how to protect yourself, we first have to pull back the curtain on the "wizard" behind the screen. For years, "Artificial Intelligence" was a buzzword found in science fiction movies about space travel and sentient robots. In 2026, it is as common as the electricity in your walls.

But there is a dark side to this miracle. Because AI can think faster than any human, it has become the ultimate tool for those who want to do harm. In this section, we aren't just looking at bits and bytes; we are looking at a fundamental shift in how the world works.

The New Landscape:

- **Chapter 1: The Invisible Hacker** – We pull back the veil on why the "rules of the game" have changed forever. No more hoodies; now it's all about algorithms.
- **Chapter 2: Meet Your Digital Double** – We break down what AI actually is. It's not a "brain", it's a pattern-matching machine that knows you better than you know yourself.

Why "Part 1" is Your Foundation

You wouldn't try to fix a car without knowing how an engine works. Similarly, you can't stay safe online without understanding the motivation and capability of an AI-powered attacker.

In this section, you will learn why the old advice like "just don't click on weird links" is no longer enough. We are moving from a world of "static" threats (things that stay the same) to "dynamic" threats (things that learn and adapt to you).

By the end of Part 1, you will stop seeing the internet as a scary, magical place and start seeing it as a system that you can master.

CHAPTER ONE

The Invisible Hacker

Imagine it's a Tuesday afternoon. The CEO of a logistics company conducts video calls with his high-ranking employee, Sarah, who attends from the company's headquarters. She can see the CEO's distinct face and sappy voice due to the coffee; he's standing in what looks like his typical home office.

"Sarah," he says, looking stressed. "We are facing difficulties with the merger. Can you please allow me to authorise an urgent $50,000 gift for our London-based legal experts? I won't do it myself since I'm boarding a plane. Can I trust you to be reliable?"

Sarah does not hesitate. She's observed him, heard him and felt his fervour. She sends the money. A post on LinkedIn ten minutes later revealed that the CEO was participating in a silent meditation retreat in Bhutan, having spent three days without a phone.

An Invisible Hacker was the one who gained Sarah's secrets. Her conversation turned out to be a Deepfake, an advanced AI system that was created to replicate anthropomorphic reality with alarming precision.

Why the Rules Have Changed.

During the past few decades, hackers were comparable to burglars who searched for an unlocked entrance. They were constrained by their own time and talent. AI has given these burglars an extraordinary power.

The "game" is transformed by AI in three significant ways.

- **Speed is key:** It could take a human hacker 3-5 days to research you. Within three seconds, an AI can examine your entire social media activity, identify your interests, and compose a personalised scam email.
- **Scale:** The scammer used to call only one person at a time. An AI bot can now make 10,000 personalised calls at the same time.
- **Precision:** AI doesn't send "Dear Customer" emails with bad grammar. By using Natural Language Processing, it can replicate human emotion and send emails that sound like those sent to your best friend or your bank.

The "Invisible Hacker" is not a person wearing a hoodie in the dark, but specialised software that learns from every single click.

Chapter 1 Key Takeaways:

Trust, but verify: Never assume a digital face or voice is real, especially when money is involved.
AI is a "Force Multiplier": It makes small-time scammers as dangerous as professional cartels.
Visuals can lie: High-quality video calls can now be faked in real time.

CHAPTER TWO

THE GRANDPARENT, THE TEEN, AND THE DEEPFAKE

Social Engineering, which involves manipulating people, has become a science-based field due to the rise of AI. AI-driven attacks bypass our logical brains by exploiting our deepest emotions, such as love, fear, and curiosity.

The Grandparent's Phone Call.

Arthur, who is sixty years old, was gardening when his phone rang. "Grandpa? It's me, Leo. I'm in trouble," the voice sobbed. It was unmistakably Leo, the same pitch, the same way he stuttered slightly when he was nervous. "I got into a car accident. I'm at the police station. I need bail money, and please don't tell Mom, she'll kill me."

Arthur was terrified. He was about to drive to the bank when his wife, Martha, stopped him. She called Leo's mobile number. Leo answered from his college dorm, safe and sound. The deceivers had employed a Voice Synthesiser. By taking just thirty seconds of audio from a video Leo posted on TikTok, the AI was able to "clone" his voice and say anything the scammer typed into a computer.

The Teen and the Social Bot.

On the other side of town, fifteen-year-old Chloe thought she was making a new friend on a gaming forum. "Jax" seemed to know everything about her favourite games and even shared her specific sense of humour.

Jax was not a boy. The training of Jax, a Large Language Model (LLM) chatbot, aimed to make it more friendly to people. Chloe received a "special game mod" from the bot after two weeks of building "trust." Despite its name, the file was malware that allowed hackers to access her laptop's webcam and all her saved passwords.

Red Flags to Watch For

While AI is beneficial, it is not flawless. To safeguard yourself, observe the "glitches in the Matrix":

- **The Emotional Hook:** A message that produces "Ultimate Fear" or "Extreme Excitement" is probably a form of manipulation.
- **Unusual Requests:** Are "untraceable gift cards" or "wire transfers" something that your grandchild would insist on?
- **Sensory Oddities:** When using video call technology, it is important to pay attention to "blurring" around the mouth or eyes, as well as to the robotic or "flat" voices when communicating with emotions.

Chapter 2 Key Takeaways:
The "Slow Down" Rule: Scammers rely on panic. If a call or message creates urgency, take a deep breath and wait five minutes.

Verify Identity: Use a different "channel" to confirm. If they text, call them. If they call, use a pre-arranged family secret.

Audio Privacy: Be mindful of sharing long clips of your voice publicly; it's the "fuel" AI needs to clone you.

CHAPTER THREE

THE EFFICIENCY ENGINE

The act of hacking was a manual skill during the internet's early days, approximately ten to fifteen years ago. If a cybercriminal wanted to break into a company or trick a person, they had to sit at a desk, type out every line of code, and manually research their targets. It was slow, tedious work. Today, that has all changed. Hacking has been transformed into an automated factory by AI.

The Hacker Who Never Sleeps.

Conceive of a telemarketer who never needs to eat, sleep, or take breaks. Suppose an ideal salesperson could converse fluently with all the languages in existence while simultaneously dialling a million phone numbers. That's the power of an AI Botnet.

A group of digital clones can be created by a single hacker in solitary confinement. The training of these AI programmes involves performing "grunt work" that was once a challenge for humans, resulting in time savings.

- **Scanning for Weakness:** Millions of websites can be scanned by AI in minutes to identify security weaknesses.
- **Cracking the Code:** To crack complex passwords, AI uses Machine Learning to predict common patterns and symbols used by people, enabling them to unlock complex ones in seconds.
- **A/B Testing Scams:** If a particular scam email is not working, the AI will automatically rewrite it, modify the subject line, and conduct another test to determine which version is more effective in tricking the intended recipients.

One Against a Thousand.

The reason behind the intense pressure caused by the emergence of cyber threats is evident. The battle has become unfair. It's not a game on the rules; it's not "you versus a hacker"; it's you versus a supercomputer that has been programmed to find your specific buttons and push them, exposing you to an indestructible supercomputer.

The "Efficiency Engine" is not solely focused on being swift; it also strives for unwavering momentum. If you ignore one fake text, the AI notes that you didn't respond and immediately tries a different angle, maybe a fake shipping notification or a "security alert" from your bank, until it finds the one that makes you click.

Why This Matters for You.

The low cost and ease of AI make hacking a target for everyone. In the past, hackers primarily targeted large-scale financial institutions or celebrities, as that was where their funds were located. A criminal can make a small profit by taking $20 from an average person, as an AI can attack 500,000 individuals for tens of thousands of dollars.

Chapter 3 Key Takeaways:

Volume is the Goal: Scammers are playing a "numbers game." They don't need everyone to fall for it, just a tiny fraction of the millions they contact.

Speed is a Weapon: If a system has a security flaw, AI will find it and exploit it before a human "good guy" even knows it exists.

Updates are Vital: Because AI is so fast at finding "holes" in software, keeping your phone and computer updated is your first line of defence. Those updates are "patches" that plug the holes that AI is looking for.

Part 2: The Weapons of Tomorrow, Today

In the past, a hacker was like a locksmith; someone with a specific set of tools who had to show up to your "digital door" and pick the lock manually. It took time, effort, and a lot of trial and error.

AI has changed the locksmith into a ghost. In this section, we go inside the hacker's high-tech workshop. We are going to look at the four primary weapons being used in 2026. These aren't just faster versions of old tricks; they are entirely new ways of attacking our trust, our voices, and even the devices we keep in our pockets. By understanding how these weapons are built, you take away their power to surprise you.

The Arsenal Overview:

- **Chapter 4: The Voice in the Shadows** – We explore Voice Cloning, where 3 seconds of audio is all an AI needs to steal your identity.
- **Chapter 5: Phishing for Perfection** – We look at Large Language Models (LLMs) that write scam emails so perfect, even an English professor couldn't spot the errors.
- **Chapter 6: The Robot Locksmith** – We see how Machine Learning predicts your password patterns before you even type them.
- **Chapter 7: When Walls Have Ears** – We go inside the Smart Home, seeing how AI bots turn your lightbulbs and cameras against you.

Why "Part 2" is the Most Important Lesson

Knowledge is the ultimate "patch" for your brain. When you understand that an AI can mimic a voice or write a perfect email, you stop reacting with emotion and start reacting with logic.

In Part 1, we learned *why* they do it. Here in Part 2, we learn *how* they do it.

CHAPTER FOUR

THE VOICE IN THE SHADOWS

The human voice served as our ultimate symbol of identity for over a century. You were aware of the person on the receiving end if you heard your husband's laughter and your best friend's "hello," in a particular tone. That sense of security has vanished in the new age of AI.

Welcome to the era of Voice Cloning.

3 Seconds is All It Takes.

In the past, to imitate someone perfectly, you had to be a world-class impressionist. A digital "mask" of your voice can be formed by hackers with only a few seconds of audio, often just three seconds in duration. Where are these snippets obtained from?

- A video you posted on social media.
- A recorded greeting on your voicemail.
- A snippet from a public speech or a gaming stream.

Having spent three seconds, the AI generates a Synthetic Voice. There is no need for the hacker to be able to speak;

instead, they can input an email into a computer and have it read by an artificial intelligence using your tone, pitch, and emotional markers.

Vishing: Phishing with a Voice.

You're familiar with the term Phishing (scam emails). This is Vishing (Voice Phishing). Because our ears are more sensitive than our eyes, these attacks are highly effective.

The use of "Deepfake-as-A-Service" increased significantly in 2025 and 2026, enabling individuals with no technical knowledge to pay for a website that replicates their work. This is particularly advantageous for criminals. However, the focus of their targeting is no longer on CEOs, but on families as well, where they are using the voice of children to demand "bail money" or a "travel emergency fund".

The "Glitch" in the Machine

Despite the intimidating nature of this, AI voices are not yet entirely satisfactory. Why? Upon close examination, it is common to hear little-known indications that the person on the line is not human.

- **The robot's lungs:** Pay attention to the way the person breathes. Artificial intelligence has difficulty with its own breathing, resulting in sentences that are too long or pauses that feel "mechanical".
- **Flat Emotions:** Emotions are typically flat, even though AI can mimic cryogenic sounds. It lacks the complexities of an actual panicked individual.
- **The "Scripted" Feel**: The AI or scammer may provide a vague and uncertain answer when you interject arbitrary questions like "What did you have for dinner last night?" This may result in an ambiguous response.

Chapter 4 Key Takeaways:

Hear with Hesitation: If a loved one calls from an unknown number with an emergency, your first instinct should be "Is this really them?" rather than "How much do they need?"

The 3-Second Rule: Be careful about posting long, clear videos of your voice publicly. The less "fuel" you give the AI, the harder you are to clone.

Ask a Random Question: Challenge the caller with a piece of personal "trivia" that isn't on the internet. "What is the name of our neighbour's dog?" can be a lifesaver.

CHAPTER FIVE

PHISHING FOR PERFECTION

A "phishing" email was a common sighting symbol in the early days of the internet. You might recall those envelopes that were filled with spelling errors, addressed to "Dear Customer," and guaranteed you a bundle of wealth from an unknown sovereign. They were the digital equivalent of a hunter throwing a giant, messy net into the ocean and hoping to catch one confused fish. The hunter has now utilised AI to replace the net with a laser-guided harpoon.

From "Spam" to "Spear-Phishing".

AI does more than just email. How? Your LinkedIn profile, your Facebook page, and your company website can be viewed by a specialised AI within seconds. The information it collects includes your work location, social connections, and writing style.

The result? A hyper-personalised phishing attack. Instead of a generic "Your account is locked" email, you might receive a message that looks like this:

"Hey [Your Name], I saw your post about the charity run last weekend. Congratulations! I noticed the receipt for your registration fee was flagged by the billing department. Could you double-check your card details here so we can finalise the donation? Thanks, [Name of a real coworker]."

The typing is not of human origin. An email sent using the Large Language Model (LLM), the same technology as helpful chatbots, is required to write a professional and friendly message to your name, providing details about their recent social media activity.

The Grammar Trap.

The rule of "check for bad grammar", making it the most effective way to detect a scam for years, has been abolished by AI. AI models are trained on billions of pages of flawless text. They are proficient in writing English, Spanish, Japanese or any other language existing in the world. The specific terminology used in your industry can also be copied by them.

Our brains tend to be less vigilant when the grammar is flawless. It appears official, so we assume it must be real.

What is the process by which AI bypasses your email filtering?

Standard spam filters scan for suspicious links or words that are "blacklisted". Despite this, AI can continuously modify the content of a fraudulent email to uncover evasive messages. This is a cat-and-mouse game in which the AI feline becomes much more agile.

Chapter 5 Key Takeaways:

Don't Trust the Tone: Just because an email sounds like a friend or looks "professional" doesn't mean it is.

The "Hover" Trick: Before clicking any link, hover your mouse over it (or long-press on a phone) to see the actual web address. If it doesn't match the official site (e.g., wellsfargo-secure-login.com instead of wellsfargo.com), it's a trap.

Go to the Source: If an email asks for info, don't click the link in the email. Close your mail app, open your browser, and type the company's address yourself.

CHAPTER SIX

THE ROBOT LOCKSMITH

A "strong" password is made up of a capital letter, a number, and some strange symbol such as an exclamation or percent sign. This has been emphasised for years by security experts. Our passwords were like P@ssw0rd123! The human eye perceives it as intricate. The act is considered humorous by an AI.

This chapter features the Robot Locksmith, which is a set of AI programmes that can guess, crack, and bypass passwords used by people for many years.

How AI "Guesses" Your Mind.

The usual hacking tools employed brute force to strike letters together, attempting to find the correct combination of letters (AAAA, AAAB, and AAAC) until it was achieved. It was slow and loud.

PassGAN (a "Generative Adversarial Network" for passwords) and other contemporary AI tools operate in a distinct manner. How does this work? They are not merely experts in the field; they also understand things. These AI models have gained insight into human thinking by examining billions of passwords that were leaked in previous data breaches. They know that:

- Most people begin with a capital letter.
- Typically, individuals add the number or emblem to their final position.
- The use of years (typically 2024 and 2025) or seasons (Summer! and Winter26) is popular.

Why? The pattern recognition capabilities of the AI allow it to crack a password that is 8 characters long and simply in less than ten minutes.

The Death of "Complexity," The Rise of "Length"

Experts have been updated by the Robot Locksmith. Our current focus is on length rather than complexity (mixing characters).

Visualise a door with an intricate lock. An AI has the capability to pick a lock with speed. Imagine having a door that is fifty miles wide? Regardless of the locksmith's proficiency, they are incapable of handling large amounts of material in a timely manner.

A complex password like Jk9#v! is much easier for an AI to crack than a lengthy passphrase, which can consist of four or five random words such as CoffeeRainBlueSky42! By adding more characters to your digital door, the thickness of it increases by millions of years.

The Ultimate Défense: Passkeys.

The length of passwords is impressive, but the aim in 2026 is to eliminate them entirely.

Enter Passkeys. Logging in through a Passkey is possible without any secret information. This is a new way to log in. Your phone or computer generates a distinct digital "key" for every website instead. Using your face, fingerprint, or device PIN is all you need to do it.

The absence of a "word" for AI to guess or steal is what makes it superior. Even if someone hacks into the website's servers, your password will remain unknown to them. What is the reason for this? Simply because no password exists.

Chapter 6 Key Takeaways:

Throw away the "8-character" rule: In the age of AI, 12 characters is the absolute minimum, but **16+ characters** are your "Digital Armour."

Switch to Passkeys: If a website (like Google, Amazon, or Apple) offers "Passkeys," take five minutes to set them up. It is the single most effective way to fire the Robot Locksmith.

Use a Password Manager: Don't try to remember 100 long passwords. Use a reputable manager (like Bitwarden, KeePass or 1Password) to generate and store "un-crackable" codes for you.

CHAPTER SEVEN

When Walls Have Ears

We've all seen the futuristic movies where a house is made to order with lights dimming when tired, the thermostat adjusting when it gets cold, and milk ordered before you even know you're gone. It's 2026, the standard Smart Home of the future, not science fiction.

But there's a catch. All "smart" devices are basically just a small computer hooked up to the internet. Your intelligent toaster is not just a tool, but also reveals secrets about you, according to an AI-armed hacker.

The Rise of the Zombie Toaster.

In the past, hackers had to manually find a way into your home network. They currently use reconnaissance bots that are powered by artificial intelligence. These robots scout the globe 24/7 for unlocked doors in the form of old software or default passwords on devices such as:

- The use of security cameras allows for monitoring your every move.
- Smart Speakers are a convenient way to listen to private conversations or passwords.

- By using Smart Plugs as a "zombie node," other devices can be targeted.

A weak device is not the sole target of an AI bot. By using your home network, a botnet can transform your device into a 'soldier' mode and target major websites or banks without you realising it.

Deepfake Voice Injection.

The most frightening new feature of 2026 is Voice Injection. Imagine your smart speaker, the one that controls your front door lock or your alarm system, hearing a voice that sounds exactly like yours.

"Alexa, unlock the front door," the voice says.

The speaker recognises your tone, your pitch, and your cadence. It clicks the lock open. The problem? You weren't the one speaking. An AI located miles away "injected" a cloned version of your voice into the room using a nearby compromised device (like a smart TV or a laptop). This is why your home needs more than just a "smart" lock; it needs a secure one.

Building Your Digital Moat.

There are no requirements to take down your smart lights. A "moat" can be formed around your virtual castle.

- **Network Segmentation:** This sounds fancy, but it's simple. Most modern routers allow you to create a **Guest Network**. Put your smart fridge, lights, and cameras on the "Guest" side, and keep your banking laptop and personal phones on the "Private" side. If a hacker gets into your lightbulb, they are "trapped" in the guest wing and can't reach your bank account.

- **The "Mute" Habit:** Many smart speakers and cameras have physical "kill switches" or sliding covers. When you're having a private family discussion or changing clothes, use them. A physical barrier is the one thing AI cannot hack.
- **Firmware is Your Shield:** Manufacturers release "Firmware Updates" to patch the holes that AI bots find. Set your devices to **Auto Update**. If a device is too old to receive updates, it's a liability; it might be time to say goodbye to that 2018 smart plug.

Chapter 7 Key Takeaways:

Treat every device like a computer: If it connects to Wi-Fi, it needs a strong, unique password and regular updates.

Use the "Guest" Network: Keep your "smart" gadgets isolated from your "sensitive" data.

Disable UPnP: Go into your router settings and turn off "Universal Plug and Play." It's a "convenience" feature that hackers love to use as an open door.

PART 3 OF "CASE STUDIES: REAL-LIFE NIGHTMARES".

After examining the tools stored in the hacker's shed, it will be interesting to see how they work. The aim of these narratives is to provide you with the clues of an AI attack, so that you can identify them in case they occur.

The study of algorithms and data packets in textbooks is one thing, but the emotional reaction to a loved one's call, making you cry, is another. In this section, we move out of the laboratory and into the living room.

The attacks presented are not solely fictional but have also led to actual attacks on individuals like you in 2025 and 2026. Walking through these scenarios will teach you to recognise the "glitch in the Matrix" before the trap springs shut. We've designed these cases to cover every generation, because AI doesn't care how old you are; it only cares if you're connected.

The Case Study Arsenal:

- **Chapter 8: The Grandchild's Cry (The Senior Citizen)** – A terrifying look at Voice Cloning. We see how a grandmother's love is weaponised through a fake kidnapping scam and how a "Safe Word" saved the day.
- **Chapter 9: The Influencer Trap (The Teenager)** – How Social Bots and Deepfake Video are used on social media to trick young people into giving up their private data or compromising photos.
- **Chapter 10: The Smart Car Stall (The Working Adult)** – A high-stakes scenario where an everyday commute turns into a digital hostage situation. We explore what happens when AI-driven IoT hacking hits the open road.

Why is "Part 3" your go-to reference point when it comes to learning?

Players watch "game film" to gain an understanding of their opponent's tactics. These chapters are your game film. It will reveal the exact location where victims felt a "gut feeling" that something was wrong, and it will also disclose the specific questions they asked to unmask the AI.

The end of this section will provide you with a thorough understanding of the threats posed by AI, including their sound, appearances, and overall mood.

CHAPTER EIGHT

THE GRANDCHILD'S CRY

Eleanor, who is 72 years old, emphasised family above all. To view pictures of her grandson, Toby, while he was at college, she kept her iPad on the kitchen counter.

On a wet Tuesday, her phone rang. When she answered it, her heart stopped racing, despite the caller ID saying "UNKNOWN Caller". The caller from the other side cried out loud, "Grandma!!!" and it was clearly Toby. "I'm so sorry. I'm in the hospital. There was a crash... the police say it's my fault because I was texting. I need $4,000 for the insurance deductible, or they won't release my car. Please don't tell Dad."

The Hook: Why Eleanor Became Angry After Finding It.

It wasn't a call made with merely an impersonator speaking in a slurpy voice. The AI had assimilated Toby's speech patterns, such as his use of "Grandma" instead of the traditional "Granny," and his voice cracking when he was upset.

The fraudulent individual utilised a Real-Time Voice Conversion programme. The AI transformed their voice into Toby's in less than a millisecond after they either typed or spoke into earphones.

The Narrow Escape.

While Eleanor was still getting her purse, she remembered the "Safe Word" that her daughter had instructed them to set up over Thanksgiving. "Toby, I'm freaking out!" Eleanor muttered with fear. "What do you think we have for our secret family snack?"

That voice, on the other end, hesitated, "Grandmother, I'm in the hospital! I'm not up for playing games! Send the funds to the link I am sending you via text."

"The snack's information would be known to Toby," Eleanor confirmed. After hanging up, she called Toby's real cell phone. He reacted from the library, bewildered but perfectly safe.

What can we learn from Eleanor?

- **The "No Secret" Rule:** Scammers often advise their victims to stay hidden from their loved ones by adhering to the "No Secret" rule, which is intended to prevent anyone from knowing about them. If someone advises you to keep a secret about money, it's not worth it.
- **The Glitch in the Panic:** Eleanor's secret inquiry was not answered by the AI Toby, who became aggressive during that moment.
- **Caller ID is a Lie:** AI fraudsters use intense emotions to prevent you from thinking rationally. Scammers can fabricate a caller ID to make it appear as if they are calling from a police station, hospital, or your own residence. Be cautious of the name on the screen.

Chapter 8 Key Takeaways:

Verify, then Act: If you receive a distress call, hang up and call that person back on their known, trusted number.

The Secret Question: Always have a piece of "offline" information that a hacker couldn't find on Facebook or Instagram.

Report It: If this happens to you, report the number to the cybersecurity cell or your local authorities. It helps them track which AI "scripts" are currently being used.

CHAPTER NINE

THE INFLUENCER TRAP

For fifteen-year-old Asmita, social media wasn't just an app; it was her digital living room. She followed dozens of "lifestyle influencers" - people who posted about fashion, gaming, and mental health.

A message arrived from Leo Vlogs, a creator with two million followers on social media, one afternoon. "Good day, Asmita! A secret giveaway for my most loyal fans. Your liking of my posts has been ongoing for months! Can I offer you a pair of limited-edition shoes for free?"

Asmita was ecstatic. The profile looked perfect. He showed up in his studio to present the latest photos and sent a video message that said, "Thank you so much, Asmita, for your support. To claim your prize, click on this link."

The Illusion: The AI "Puppet Master"

But Asmita was not talking to Leo. It was a social bot powered by a Deepfake video generator. In 2026, hackers don't just steal photos; they "animate" them. They took a real video of Leo, used AI to change what his mouth was saying (called Lip-Syncing), and used a cloned version of his voice to say Asmita's name. To a teenager staring at a small phone screen, it looked 100% real.

Through the "prize link," a fake login page that looked like Instagram was created. Asmita entered the username and password to authenticate herself. Within seconds, the hackers had:

- Locked her out of her account.
- Scammed her friends by sending them the same "giveaway" link from her trusted profile.
- Accessed her private photos, threatening to leak them unless she paid a "ransom" in cryptocurrency.

The "Tells" of a Digital Puppet.

Despite her intelligence, Asmita was always too quick to react. You must never be fast while engaging with an AI. She might have noticed the signs of Social Engineering if she had slowed down:

- **The "Too Good to be True" Offer:** DMs from famous influencers to random followers are not common for offering expensive items. This is a rare opportunity.
- **The "Urgency" Tactic:** Using the "Urgency" tactic, the bot gave her a brief opportunity to claim the prize within ten minutes before it was given to someone else. This is meant to prevent you from thinking logically.
- **The URL Glitch:** Instagram's URL was not credible as it was not instagram.com, but rather as instagr-am-secure.net. A minor discrepancy that cost her everything.

Escaping the Trap.

Asmita's parents and the platform's security team were instrumental in helping her retrieve her account, but it was a painful experience. She felt violated by a machine that was aware of her identity and interests.

Chapter 9 Key Takeaways:

Verify the Checkmark: Even a "Blue Check" can be faked, or an account can be hacked. If a celebrity DMs you out of the blue, treat it with extreme suspicion.

Never "Re-Login": If a link asks you to enter your password for a site you are *already* logged into, close the app. It's almost certainly a **Phishing** site.

Two-Factor Authentication (2FA): If Asmita had 2FA turned on (where you need a code from your phone to log in), the hackers couldn't have gotten into her account even with her password.

CHAPTER TEN

The Smart Car Stall

It was 8:15 a.m. on a Monday. In his stylish, electric SUV, Marcus, a 42-year-old software sales rep, was driving down the street. His vehicle was a masterpiece of 2026 technology, featuring "Autopilot Lite," an enormous touchscreen instrument panel, and uninterrupted 5G connectivity for real-time traffic updates.

Suddenly, the music cut out. The dashboard display flashed in a bright red hue. A voice that was artificial intelligence and mechanical echoed through the car's high-quality speakers: "Emergency Protocol Initiated. Vehicle Control Overridden."

The steering wheel became stiff before Marcus could respond. It started to slow down without him using his foot on the gas until it came to a stop in an alleyway. The doors clicked. Locked.

The Ransom on Wheels.

It read: "Your vehicle's software has been encrypted." To regain control of the doors, you must send 0.05 Bitcoin to the address below. The climate control will shut off after 20 minutes.

Marcus wasn't a victim of a mechanical failure. He was a victim of **Automated Exploitation**.

An AI "Stalker Bot" was examining thousands of vehicles on the road in pursuit of a specific Zero-Day Vulnerability, which the car manufacturer had not disclosed. Upon discovering Marcus's car, the AI did not require an individual to communicate with it. Using its cellular entertainment system, the ransom software was automatically instigated.

The Digital Kidnapping.

The most frightening aspect of the "New Age" is the fact that hackers infringed on your data. Our cars, ovens and medical devices are smart enough to steal our physical freedom. Marcus's identity was inconsequential to the AI. It just knew that a person stuck on a highway in a $70,000 car is very likely to pay a few hundred dollars to get moving again. It was a "low-effort, high-reward" attack for the criminal, handled entirely by a computer program.

How Marcus Handled the "Stall"

Marcus did not pay. He knew that paying a digital kidnapper would pay for itself in the event of another AI attack. He chose to call the car manufacturer's emergency roadside assistance using his phone, which was on a different network. A "Hard Reset" was sent to the car's computer by them.

The result?

Despite being late for an hour, he did not succumb to the "Robot Ransom" challenge.

Chapter 10 Key Takeaways:

The "Offline" Backup: Always have a physical way to exit your vehicle (like a manual door release handle) and a separate way to communicate (your cell phone) that isn't tied to the car's dashboard.

Software Updates are Safety Updates: When your car or "Smart Home" app says it needs an update, do it immediately. These updates are often "digital armour" against the latest AI scanning bots.

Don't Pay the Ransom: Statistics show that people who pay "Digital Ransoms" are 80% more likely to be targeted again because the AI marks them as a "Ready Payer."

PART 4: YOUR DIGITAL ARMOUR.

You've seen the weapons. You've heard the stories. You must now take your hat off. We discussed how AI can become a predator in the previous sections.

We shift the focus in Part 4. Our presentation will delve into how to use basic habits, technologically advanced techniques, and AI to create a defence that is too challenging for any hacker.

Additionally, there will be explanations on what not to do. The hacker's AI is seeking an uncomplicated victory, but if you follow the instructions provided in this section, you will end up as a "hard target."

Your Defensive Arsenal:

- **Chapter 11: The Family Safe Word** – We've already built our first line of defence: the "analogue" secret that no AI can guess.
- **Chapter 12: Spotting the Glitch** – You will learn to become a "Deepfake Detective." We'll show you the tiny visual and auditory errors that AI still makes, like "floating" glasses, weird shadows, or unnatural blinking.
- **Chapter 13: Fighting Fire with Fire** – We explore AI-powered Security. Learn how to use modern antivirus and email filters that use their own "Good AI" to hunt down and block the "Bad AI" before it reaches your screen.
- **Chapter 14: The Human Firewall** – The final piece of the puzzle. We'll discuss the "Mindset of Scepticism", how to stay calm, stay curious, and stay safe in an age where seeing is no longer believing.

Why "Part 4" is Your Victory Lap

Security isn't about being a computer expert; it's about maintaining consistency. You can dodge the AI, but you must be more prepared than the millions of people who are not reading this book.

You will not feel powerless after finishing these chapters. Your phone, home, and family will be protected with a comprehensive checklist provided. You are transitioning from a "target" to a "protector."

CHAPTER ELEVEN

THE FAMILY SAFE WORD

In an era where a computer can mimic your daughter's sob or your husband's frantic request for help, we must return to a very "low-tech" solution to solve a "high-tech" problem. This is the Family Safe Word.

Think of a safe word as a digital handshake. It is a secret piece of information that only your inner circle knows. If someone calls you claiming to be a family member in distress, and they can't produce the safe word, you know instantly that the "person" on the other end is an AI-generated fake.

Step 1: The Selection Process.

- **Don't use:** Avoid including birthdays, pet names, your street address, or any other content shared on social media. The information can be found by AI in a matter of seconds.
- **Do use:** It is recommended to use either a random combination of two unconnected words or reminisce about 'inside jokes' from the past.
- **Examples:** "Blue Pineapple," "Toasted Marshmallow," or "Grandpa's Rusty Tractor."

Step 2: Implement the "Distress Protocol".

Collaborate with your family, including children and grandparents, to determine the appropriate time to use the safe word.

- **The Rule:** In the event of a caller asking for money, passwords, or personal assistance from an unidentified number or their own number, the receiver must disclose their family code.
- **The Response:** The caller must provide the word as soon as possible. Stopping a Social Engineering attack by using excuses ("I am too busy to remember!") or hanging up. Is this what works so well?

Step 3: The "Out-of-Band" Verification.

The third stage involves verifying the accuracy of "Out-of-Band" information. Don't engage the caller or argue if they don't answer back with the safe word test.

- Hang up immediately.
- Use the saved phone number in your contacts to call the person who called you.
- Utilise a secondary app like WhatsApp or Instagram to send incoming messages and check for responses from the recipient.

Step 4: Maintenance.

Your safe word should be inspected periodically, just like a smoke detector battery. Use the phrase during a festive gathering or through text messaging to keep it in your thoughts. You can change the word immediately if you suspect it has been "leaked," for example, if you spoke to someone over an unencrypted Wi-Fi connection.

Chapter 11 Key Takeaways:

Keep it Offline: Never text your safe word or email it. Tell it to your family members in person.

No Exceptions: Teach children that even if the "caller" sounds exactly like Mom or Dad, they must ask for the code if the request is unusual.

Simplicity is Strength: You don't need fancy software to beat a billion-dollar AI; you just need a secret that isn't on the internet.

CHAPTER TWELVE

SPOTTING THE GLITCH.

In movies, the "imposter" is commonly exposed as they either cannot remember their middle name or act out of character. By 2026, the AI equivalent is far more disciplined. It stores your social media activity, coffee preferences, and conversation frequency.

The concept of AI is not a human being but rather based on mathematical principles. "Artificial" digital scars that prove the non-existence of the image, video, or voice being viewed can be found even in the most sophisticated math equations. You must become a Deepfake Detective to ensure your safety.

The Video "Tells".

Despite the fact that AI models like Sora and Veo have made video realistic by 2026, they still struggle with conveying the "physical aspects of human" behaviour. These specific glitches are worth keeping an eye on:

- **The "Mechanical" Blink:** Humans use a "Mechanical" blink, which occurs spontaneously every 2 to 10 seconds. The gaze of AI faces can either be prolonged without blinking for an unnatural amount or produce a heavy-coloured glow that resembles lead eyelids.

- **The shadow gap:** Pay attention to the neck and ears. The movement of an AI-generated person's head often results in unclear shadows. It is possible to observe shadow flickering or a jawline that seems to blend into the shirt collar.
- **The Jewellery Warp:** Consistent detail is a hindrance for AI in areas like the Jewellery Warp. Watch closely for the person's movement if they have earrings or glasses on. Do the earrings change shape? Does the frame of the glasses "blur" into the skin near the temple?
- **The Blocky Smile:** Examine the teeth for any obstructions. Deepfakes frequently exhibit teeth that resemble a single, solid white block instead of individual teeth.

The Audio "Tells ".

- **The Room Echo:** AI clones often sound "too clean." If a family member is calling from a supposed "car crash" or a "busy airport," but their voice sounds like they are in a professional recording studio with zero background noise, be suspicious.
- **Unnatural Breathing:** Artificial Intelligence does not require the ability to breathe. Examine for gaps in breathing, such as when a word is about to be written or when someone expresses their emotions in an emotional sentence.
- **Unnatural Breathing:** Real-time AIs can experience latency or a one-second delay when faced with an unexpected question.

The Text "Tells ".

Look for The AI Voice when reading a DM or email.

- **The "Wikipedia" Tone:** A message with a tone that is highly balanced, punctuation-conscious, and often lowercase would be considered suspicious if it were to be sent by slang-speaking friends.
- **The Rule of Three:** AI prioritises lists of three, as per the Rule of Three. This statement is urgent, crucial, and imperative, while humans tend to be more haphazard.
- **Hallucinations:** AI sometimes makes up facts with total confidence. If an email mentions a "mutual friend" or a specific "past event" that never happened, the AI is "hallucinating" (guessing based on a pattern).
- **The "Deepfake Detection Checklist":** includes icons for Eyes (Blinking), Ears (Background Noise), and Hands (Physics/Movement).

The "Occlusion " Test.

If you are on a video call and suspect a deepfake, try the Hand Test. Ask the person to wave their hand directly in front of their face. Most real-time deepfake models struggle when an object (like a hand or a pen) "covers" the face. The digital mask will often flicker, distort, or disappear for a split second.

Chapter 12 Key Takeaways:

Trust Your Gut: If something feels "waxy," "robotic," or "off," it probably is. Our brains have evolved to recognise human life; trust that instinct.

Look for Physics: AI is great at "looking" like a person but bad at "behaving" like one. Watch for things that defy gravity or anatomy.

Metadata Checks: In 2026, many browsers have "C2PA" tools (like the Content Authenticity button). If an image is AI-generated, these tools can often "read" the digital watermark hidden in the file.

CHAPTER THIRTEEN

FIREFIGHTING WITH FIRE.

It's possible that you feel like you're in for a knife during armed gun battles. What are the ways for an average individual to survive when hackers are utilising super-intelligent AI to disrupt their work?

The simple answer is to produce your own AI.

A battle between AI and AI has developed over the last two years with the aim of addressing cybersecurity. Just like how hackers rely on machine learning to identify vulnerabilities, security companies use Defensive AI to act as a digital bodyguard that can detect scams at any time and without fail.
1. Your AI Bodyguard (Modern Antivirus)

By utilising Behavioural AI, modern antiviruses like Norton 360, Bitdefender, and McAfee's Deepfake Detector can eliminate the need for outdated antivirus software that only searches for bad files. Instead of waiting for a known virus to appear, these devices are utilised as surveillance tools.

Scandal: You've unintentionally downloaded a file that looks like.

Damage Control: Your AI bodyguard becomes aware that the file is trying to access your saved passwords, which is not advisable for PDFs. Before it can cause harm, the AI immediately "freezes" the file and deletes it.

2. The Smart Filter (AI Email & SMS Protection)

The "perfect" phishing email can be created by AI, as demonstrated in Chapter 5. Google and Microsoft have resorted to using Natural Language Classifiers to combat this issue. These are "Good AI" models trained to recognise the subtle patterns of a scam. They are not only searching for weak links, but also for the message's intended meaning. Your "bank" email is flagged by an AI as "High Risk" if it uses a more aggressive tone or asks for data in an unusual way, before you can even access your inbox. This happens frequently.

3. Fighting the Fakes: Deepfake Detectors.

One of the most fascinating things in your 2026 armour is a Real-Time Deepfake Validator.

- **Browser Extensions:** Digimarc and CloudSEK, two browser extensions, can now scan your video and provide a "Truth Score." If they detect that someone has been digitally altered, if you watch their face, it will display smudge marks in the upper right-hand corner of your screen.
- **Authentication Standards (C2PA):** The "Content Credentials" icon, a small 'cr' symbol, is frequently seen on images and videos to comply with C2PA. A digital seal of authenticity is provided, which proves that the media was obtained from an actual camera and has not been altered by artificial intelligence.

4. Biometric "Liveness" Checks.

Using either a picture of your face or voice recordings, hackers could potentially trick your phone. Liveness Detection is employed by 2026 devices to prevent this from occurring. The AI doesn't solely observe your face but instead concentrates on microscopic movements such as light-emitting pupils or skin pulses. Keeping your phone locked is essential when an AI-generated photo or video attempts to fake biological "micro-signals".

Chapter 13. Key Takeaways:

Enable "Autopilot" Features: Most modern security software has an AI "Autopilot" mode. Turn it on. It allows the software to make split-second decisions to block threats without waiting for you to click "Yes."

Use AI-Powered Browsing: Use extensions that block "Newly Registered Domains." Since scammers create thousands of websites a day, your AI can block any site that was created less than 24 hours ago, a common trait of a scam.

Update for the AI: The "Good AI" gets smarter every day, but only if you download the latest updates. Think of an update as a "brain transplant" for your security software.

CHAPTER FOURTEEN

THE HUMAN FIREWALL.

We've reached the boundary of your digital protection. Our discussions have centred on passwords, AI-generated antivirus, and uncovering deepfakes. There is only one security system that cannot be fully replaced by software, and it is your own mind. This is referred to as the **“Human Firewall”** in the future of cybersecurity. Despite using AI against machines, hackers typically depend on humans to make mistakes, such as clicking a button, sending an email, or listening to voices.

A "**Human Firewall**" is not a tech-savvy individual. Why? It's about creating a specific reflex to protect you in case the machines fail.

Using The Universal Reflex, you can "feel" and "act" at the same time. Your emotional state is the primary focus of an AI attack, not your computer. To conquer it, you must adopt this four-step routine:

- **FEEL:** Notice your emotions. Am I feeling panicked? Am I suddenly very excited? Does this message make me feel guilty? The first indication of concern is emotion.
- **SLOW:** Rapidity is the preferred preference of scammers and AI bots. They want you to do it now before your logic runs out. Take a deep breath. Count to ten. A pause of up to sixty seconds is available in real emergencies.

- **VERIFY:** Avoid trusting the message's intended recipient. You can reach out to them by calling them. Use a secure term or an alternative app if they call you. Go "out-of-band" to confirm.
- **ACT:** Only after receiving 100% confirmation should you proceed with the ACT. In case of doubt, eliminate it and report it.

The benefits of embracing "healthy scepticism":

In the "New Age," we must switch from "Trust" to "Verify." While it may appear cynical, it's a powerful tool.

- **The New Rule of Sight:** "Seeing is no longer believing." If a video call feels "off," it probably is.
- **The New Rule of Sound:** "Hearing is no longer proof." If a voice asks for money or a password, it's a "voice until proven otherwise."

Your Family's "Security Culture":

The strongest Human Firewall is one that works together.

- **Talk about it:** Make cybersecurity a normal dinner table conversation, not a scary "taboo" topic.
- **Reward Reporting:** If a child or a grandparent clicks a bad link, don't get angry. If people are afraid of being blamed, they will hide the mistake, which gives the hacker more time to do damage. Instead, celebrate the fact that they told you so you can fix it together.

Conclusion: You're the Shield.

The era of AI offers remarkable potential in terms of language learning, art creation, and problem-solving. There are endless possibilities! But like every great tool in history, it can be used as a weapon. Like nuclear energy that can be used for the progression of mankind, the same nuclear power can also be used for the destruction of the world.

You have transitioned from being a spectator to essentially observing and participating. You possess knowledge on the "Why, How and Why," as well as your defence mechanisms, AI-generated tools (such as time machines), and a critical yet sceptical mindset.

Despite their speed, the Invisible Hacker is lazy. Why? They are seeking the "open window." By closing your digital doors and staying vigilant, you are not only protecting your data but also your family, finances, and peace of mind.

Chapter 14. Key Takeaways:

Emotion = Risk: If a digital message makes you feel a strong emotion, it is time to slow down.

Be the "Coach," Not the "Critic": Help your family members learn from mistakes instead of punishing them.

Stay Curious: The world of AI changes every week. Keep reading, keep asking questions, and keep your "Digital Armour" updated.

www.ingramcontent.com/pod-product-compliance
Lightning Source LLC
LaVergne TN
LVHW101617210926
848480LV00009B/774